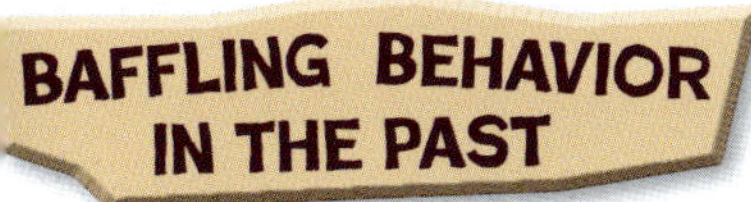

by Noah Leatherland

Minneapolis, Minnesota

Credits

Images are courtesy of Shutterstock.com. With thanks to Getty Images, Thinkstock Photo, and iStockphoto. COVER & RECURRING – Feliks Kogan, JORDEN MARBLE, Sabelskaya, Nsit, Siberian Art. 4–5 – Russ Heinl, n_defender. 6–7 – Design Musketeer, n_defender, Aastels. 8–9 – NataliAlba, BMJ. 10–11 – Svetliy, AB Photographie, Scott E Read. 12–13 – Martin Christopher Parker, evaurban, Elena Platova, Chinch. 14–15 – LGieger, Little_Monster_2070, Sylfida. 16–17 – Ovchinnikova Irina, lindasky76. 18–19 – Rawpixel.com, Designer things, Signed "H. L. M.", Public domain, via Wikimedia Commons, Cristian Kirshbom. 20–21 – Sanne Romijn Fotografie, GoodStudio. 22–23 – keeble1337, Lorenz Frølich, Public domain, via Wikimedia Commons, Ksenia Zezyukina. 24–25 – Helga Miller, NataliAlba. 26–27 – LGieger, Sergey Didenko. 28–29 – Johannes Flintoe, Public domain, via Wikimedia Commons, Sacrificial scene on Hammars (II).png, CC BY-SA 4.0 <https://creativecommons.org/licenses/by-sa/4.0>, via Wikimedia Commons. 30–31 – Zimneva Natalia.

Bearport Publishing Company Product Development Team

Publisher: Jen Jenson; Director of Product Development: Spencer Brinker; Managing Editor: Allison Juda; Editor: Cole Nelson; Associate Editor: Naomi Reich; Associate Editor: Tiana Tran; Art Director: Colin O'Dea; Designer: Kim Jones; Designer: Kayla Eggert; Product Development Specialist: Owen Hamlin

Library of Congress Cataloging-in-Publication Data is available at www.loc.gov or upon request from the publisher.

ISBN: 979-8-89232-883-8 (hardcover)
ISBN: 979-8-89232-969-9 (paperback)
ISBN: 979-8-89232-913-2 (ebook)

For more information, write to Bearport Publishing, 5357 Penn Avenue South, Minneapolis, MN 55419.

CONTENTS

THE VIKING AGE

Life in the Viking Age was full of rich history . . . and baffling behavior! Looking back, some of the stories we hear from the Viking Age may seem strange.

The Viking Age took place from around 800 to 1066 CE. The Vikings were famous for traveling to faraway places and making homes wherever they went.

CE MEANS COMMON ERA. THIS IS THE TIME AFTER THE YEAR 0.

In the past, Scandinavia was home to the **Norse** people. Those Norse people who traveled and settled in other places became known as Vikings.

Many people think of Vikings as only wild individuals. But the Vikings were also very smart. Their **civilization** was just as interesting and as baffling as many others in history.

THE GODS AND THE REALMS

The Vikings believed in many different gods and goddesses. They claimed each one looked after a different part of life.

YGGDRASIL

Vikings thought there were nine different worlds called realms. Earth was a realm called Midgard. Another realm, Asgard, was home to the gods. All nine worlds were connected by a giant tree called Yggdrasil (IG-drah-sil).

The Vikings believed in an **afterlife**. They thought most people went to a realm called Helheim when they died.

Warriors who died in battle were thought to go to Valhalla. There, all the dead warriors would have a feast with Odin, the king of the gods. They would eat, drink, and join Odin's army.

RAIDERS, TRADERS, AND EXPLORERS

Many of the Norse people who lived in Scandinavia were farmers. Others worked with metal, wood, and fabrics.

However, some of the Norse wanted more land and money. So, they went on **raids**. These Vikings attacked places that had lots of gold and riches, such as **monasteries**.

Vikings were not just raiders. They were also traders. Vikings would buy from and sell to the people they met on their long travels.

Leif Eriksson was a Viking explorer. Around 1000 CE, Eriksson sailed from Greenland to North America. He became the first person from Europe to land there.

GOING BERSERK

The Vikings were known as fierce warriors. Some loved to fight more than others. Berserkers were warriors that people thought had a magical connection to certain animals.

When berserkers got into fights, they were said to act strangely. The warriors would get worked up and lose control of themselves.

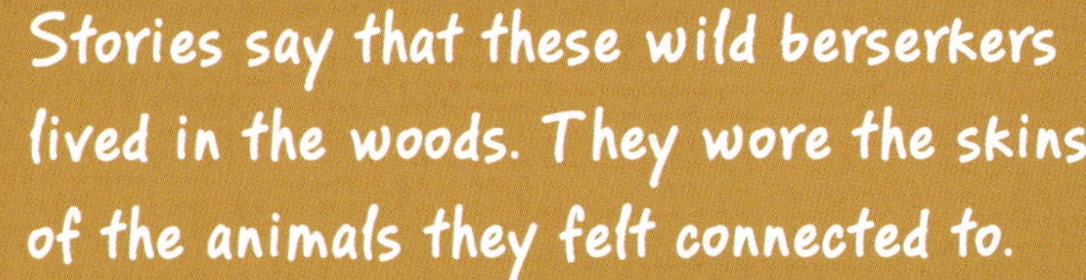

Stories say that these wild berserkers lived in the woods. They wore the skins of the animals they felt connected to.

Not all berserkers acted the same. Wolf berserkers barked and howled, just as wolves do. Bear berserkers were very dangerous. They attacked anyone that came near them.

PETS OF THE PAST

Many Vikings kept pets. Like today, dogs were the most common pet. They helped their owners hunt and guard their homes.

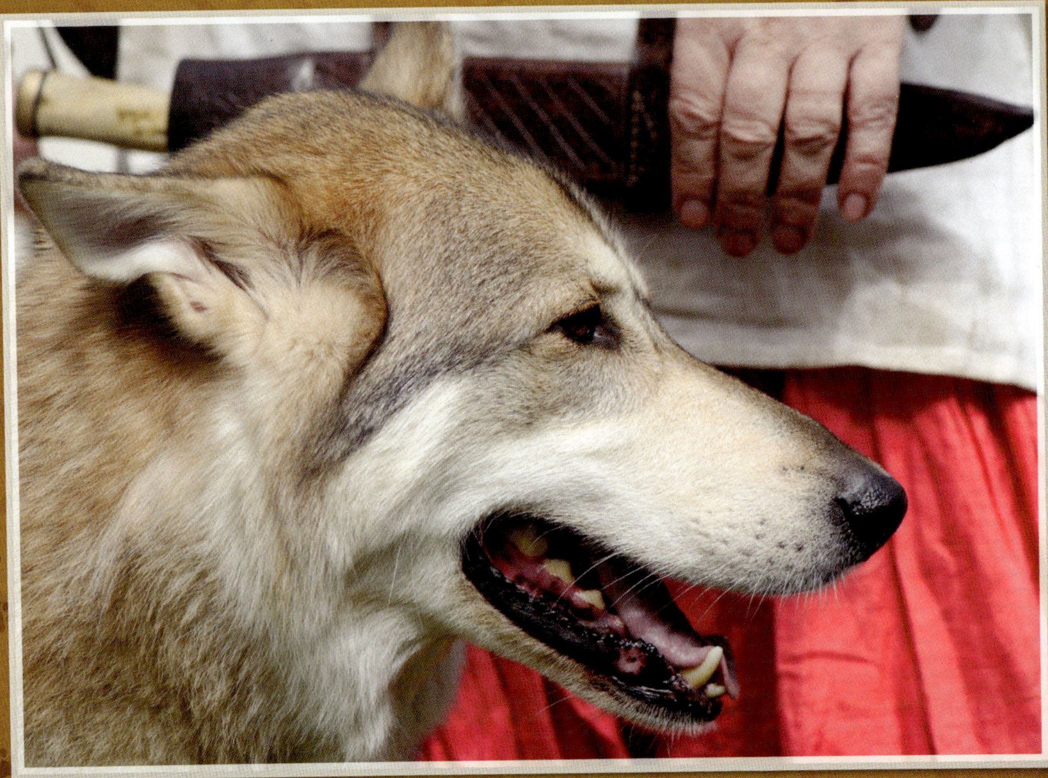

Some Vikings even took their dogs with them on raids. They believed that some brave dogs could make it to Valhalla in the afterlife.

There were also some dangerous pets in the Viking Age. Some people found baby bears in the wild and took them home. Sometimes, the bears were tame after a while. However, a lot of them caused trouble.

Rich Viking rulers sometimes kept even fancier pets. They had people sail to the Arctic to bring polar bears back for them.

PRETTY VIKINGS

Vikings cared a lot about looking good. Many men wanted light-colored hair. They used special shampoo on their hair and beards to turn them blond.

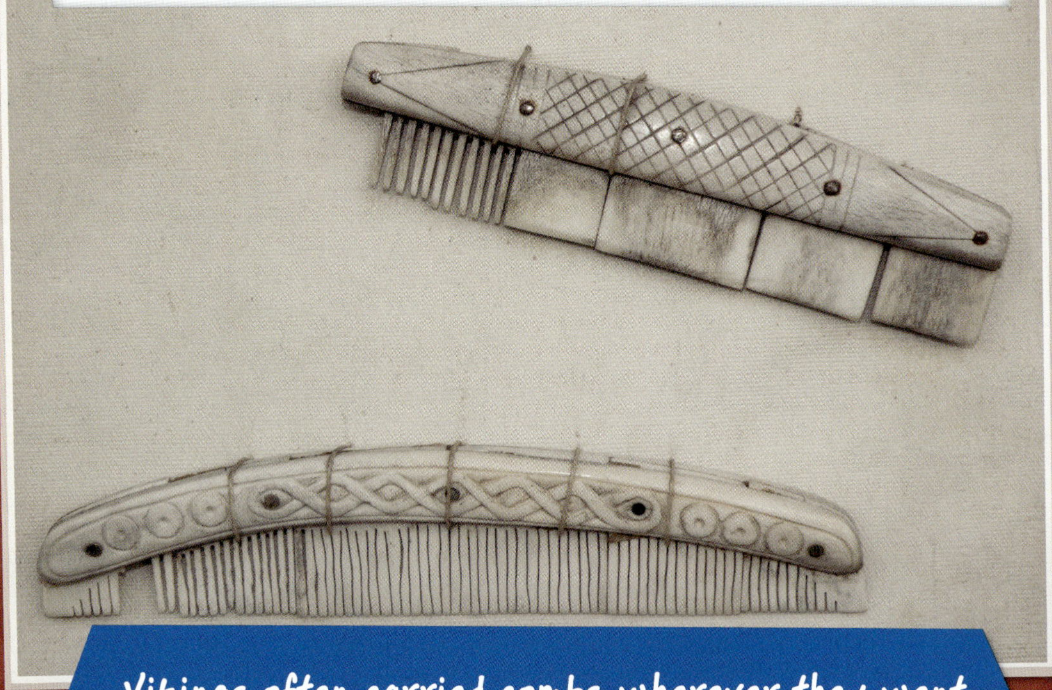

Vikings often carried combs wherever they went to make sure their hair always looked nice. Some people were buried with their combs. Perhaps they wanted to look pretty even in the afterlife.

Most women grew their hair long and tied it up. Some men had such pretty hair that it became part of their names.

Despite what we may think of today, most Vikings' helmets did not have horns. But what the Vikings did have was decorated teeth. Some people cut lines into them!

SQUEAKY CLEAN

People throughout history could get pretty dirty. However, Vikings kept themselves much cleaner than others. They bathed about once a week. Others who lived at the same time may have bathed only once a year!

VIKINGS BATHED IN HOT SPRINGS.

Vikings also made sure to clean their ears. They made little spoons out of bones to scoop wax out.

FIRE STARTERS

Vikings needed fires when they camped. They found a way of starting a fire with their pee!

TINDER MUSHROOM

First, Vikings cut up and burned tinder mushrooms. Then, they boiled these mushroom bits in a pot of pee. The boiled bits were taken on journeys and used to start fires.

DO NOT TRY THIS YOURSELF!

PLAYING GAMES

Vikings created a lot of dangerous games. One swimming game involved holding another player underwater for as long as possible. If you were to drown, it was seen as your own fault.

Like today, Vikings also played tug-of-war. However, they played it over a fire. Whoever was pulled toward the fire lost . . . and risked being burned!

DO NOT TRY THESE VIKING GAMES!

Vikings often lived in very cold places. When there was snow, they used wooden skis to get around. Sometimes, Vikings hunted while skiing down hills.

Skating over ice was not a problem for Vikings. They stuck animal bones to the bottom of their shoes. Then, they used sticks to push themselves over frozen lakes.

RUNES

Vikings wrote using runes. Runes were shapes that could be **carved** into things. Each rune **represented** a different sound.

F U TH A R K G W

H N I J OR Y P Z S T

B E M L NG O D

The people believed Odin discovered runes. They also thought each rune was magical. The Vikings claimed carving a rune on their weapons could make them stronger in battle.

Vikings thought that some people could use the magic of the runes. Runes would be carved onto small pieces of wood, bone, or stone. Then, they would be given to women called seeresses.

RUNES CARVED INTO STONES

According to Viking stories, a seeress could use the runes to see into the future as well as heal or curse people.

FEASTING TIME

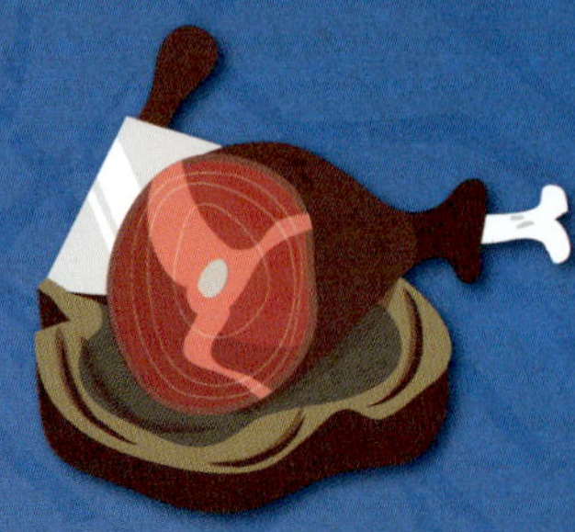

When it was time to celebrate, Vikings put on huge feasts. People gathered in a building called a longhouse. Inside, there were long tables for all the food and drinks.

To make the gods happy, Vikings **sacrificed** animals before feasts. If a Viking wanted to show that they loved the gods, they might even sacrifice their best horse.

Vikings entertained one another with games, including one called flyting. Flyting was all about coming up with the best insults.

A DRAWING OF NORSE GODS FLYTING

This game was not about just being rude. If a player wanted to win, they had to make sure their insults were also clever and sounded **poetic**.

KIDS DID WHAT?

Life was tough for children in the Viking Age. Some stories say that if parents did not think their babies were strong enough, they just threw them away!

Most Vikings lived on farms. Their homes did not have many rooms. Viking families kept a fire in the middle of the house. Everyone slept on benches around the fire.

Viking children did not go to school. Their parents taught them everything they needed to know at home. Children learned how to make things, how to cook, and how to work on farms.

Most children were also taught how to fight with swords, spears, and axes. Once they got older, they went out on raids.

BREAKING THE LAW

Vikings did not have police to help stop crimes. Instead, most Vikings settled things on their own by fighting one another.

Sometimes, Vikings gathered in big meetings to decide what to do with **criminals**. Most criminals just had to pay a fine. However, some had much worse punishments.

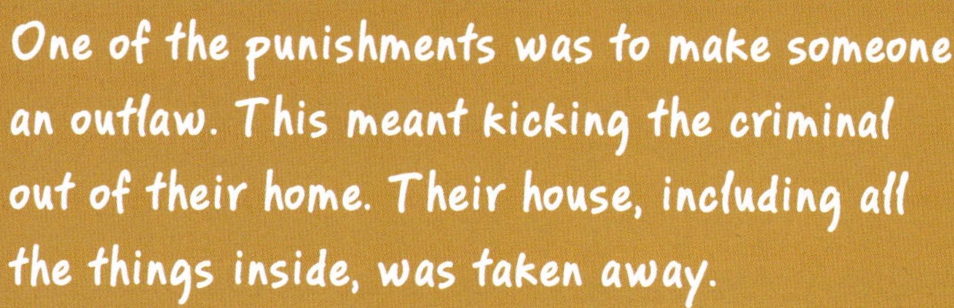

One of the punishments was to make someone an outlaw. This meant kicking the criminal out of their home. Their house, including all the things inside, was taken away.

Life as an outlaw could be very dangerous. As the name suggests, an outlaw was outside the law. Other Vikings could kill someone who was an outlaw and not get into trouble!

BATTERED AND BLOODY

Many Vikings sorted out arguments with a fight called a holmgang. The Vikings believed the gods were on the side of whoever won the holmgang.

A HOLMGANG

Sometimes, holmgangs ended when someone started to bleed. Other times, it was a fight to the death!

Vikings had some very **brutal** punishments for crimes. One punishment was called the blood eagle. It involved peeling the skin on a criminal's back to look like wings. First, the person had their back cut open. Then, their ribs were pulled out. *Ouch!*

YOUR PLACE IN HISTORY

Do you think you could live in the Viking Age? From fighting to the death to decorating your teeth, the people who lived in the past sure had it rough.

If you think being in the Viking Age was tough, then try reading about another time period. However, be warned! Wherever you go, you may find yourself thinking . . .

what baffling behavior!

GLOSSARY

afterlife the life of a person after their death

brutal extremely tough or difficult

carved cut into a shape or form

civilization a large group of people that shares the same history or way of life

criminals people who break the law

monasteries religious buildings that are home to monks or nuns

Norse having to do with ancient or medieval Scandinavia

poetic like a song or a poem

raids sudden attacks made with the goal of taking valuable things

represented stood for something else

sacrificed killed an animal in order to please a god or gods

INDEX

READ MORE

Kerry, Isaac. *Science on Viking Expeditions (The Science of History).* North Mankato, MN: Capstone Press, 2023.

Troupe, Thomas Kingsley. *Savage Vikings (Ancient Warriors).* New York: Crabtree Publishing, 2024.

LEARN MORE ONLINE

1. Go to **FactSurfer.com** or scan the QR code below.

2. Enter "**Life in the Viking Age**" into the search box.

3. Click on the cover of this book to see a list of websites.